MW01012498

To

From

Date

The MAJESTY *of* PRAYER

JOHN MACARTHUR

Photography by DENNIS FRATES

HARVEST HOUSE PUBLISHERS

EUGENE, OREGON

The MAJESTY of PRAYER

Text copyright © 2012 by John MacArthur
Photography copyright © 2012 by Dennis Frates

Published by Harvest House Publishers
Eugene, Oregon 97402
www.harvesthousepublishers.com

ISBN 978-0-7369-3841-9

For more information about Dennis Frates, contact
International Artist Management Group
Linda Mariano
1.408.718.3730

Design and production by Left Coast Design, Portland, Oregon

Prayers for this book are taken from *At the Throne of Grace* by John MacArthur, Harvest House
Publishers, 2011.

Harvest House Publishers has made every effort to trace the ownership of all poems and quotes. In
the event of a question arising from the use of a poem or quote, we regret any error made and will be
pleased to make the necessary correction in future editions of this book.

All Scripture quotations are taken from the New American Standard Bible®, © 1960, 1962, 1963, 1968,
1971, 1972, 1973, 1975, 1977, 1995 by The Lockman Foundation. Used by permission.
(www.Lockman.org)

This quotation from D. Martyn Lloyd-Jones is used with the permission of the MLJ Recordings Trust
(United Kingdom): "The Christian life starts with grace, it must continue with grace, it ends with grace.
Grace, wondrous grace."

Printed in China

12 13 14 15 16 17 18 19 20 / FC / 10 9 8 7 6 5 4 3 2 1

A Word from
John MacArthur

—◇◇◇—

As children of God, we are encouraged to come into God's presence and through prayer talk to our heavenly Father: "Let us draw near with confidence to the throne of grace, so that we may receive mercy and find grace to help in time of need" (Hebrews 4:16). Through prayer we talk to God Himself. We open our hearts to Him in search of guidance, strength, and comfort...and we praise and thank Him for His gifts of goodness and grace.

My heart's desire is that the prayers in this volume will inspire you toward more intimate communion with God, and will stir you to a heartfelt gratitude for the blessings He richly makes available to you.

Delighting in God

The precepts of the L{ORD} are right, rejoicing the heart;
The commandment of the L{ORD} is pure, enlightening the eyes.

PSALM 19:8

Precious heavenly Father, all our delight is in You.

The deepest longing of our hearts is to see and to celebrate Your glory.

We will not be truly satisfied

until we behold Your face in righteousness.

That is why we now pour out our love and worship to You in prayer.

We trust in Your promises,

rejoice in Your faithfulness,

glory in Your goodness,

hope in Your Word,

believe in Your Son,

and rest in Your grace.

—◇◇◇◇◇—

Thank You for enabling us to rest in full assurance.

We know that past, present, and future are all in Your care.

We joyfully confess that Your plan is best,

      Your commandments are just,

      Your wisdom is flawless,

      Your power is supreme,

      and all Your ways are perfect.

You are full of lovingkindness, merciful, holy, upright, and gracious—

      the fountain of all that is truly good.

—◇◇◇◇◇—

Be not afraid of saying too much in the praises of God;
all the danger is of saying too little.

MATTHEW HENRY

—◇◇◇◇◇—

Every work of God serves to display His glory,
and set off the greatness of His majesty.

JOHN GILL

All Thy works with joy surround Thee, earth and heaven reflect Thy rays,
Stars and angels sing around Thee, center of unbroken praise.
Field and forest, vale and mountain, flowery meadow, flashing sea,
Singing bird and flowing fountain call us to rejoice in Thee.

HENRY VAN DYKE

God's Kind of Love

Beloved, let us love one another, for love is from God;
and everyone who loves is born of God and knows God.

1 JOHN 4:7

We thank You for loving us into Your family and kingdom.

As we come before You now, fill us with that heavenly love

  so that our worship will be a foretaste of true heavenly praise.

Give us Christlike love for one another—

  the love that takes up towel and basin

    and gladly serves in the lowliest place.

Give us grace to render that service and sacrifice

  with overflowing joy and true humility.

Empower us to encourage and love one another

  and give of ourselves freely, just as Christ did for us.

May we see beyond the faces of those whom we serve—

  as blessed, beloved, and precious as they may be—

  and may we look to You, the One whom we are to love

    with all our heart, soul, mind, and strength.

God's love is always supernatural, always a miracle,
always the last thing we deserve.
ROBERT HORN

Love is swift, sincere, pious, joyful, generous, strong, patient, faithful,
prudent, long-suffering, courageous, and never seeking its own; for
wheresoever a person seeketh his own, there he falleth from love.
THOMAS À KEMPIS

There is nothing little in God.

C.H. SPURGEON

His Mercies
Endure Forever

The Lord is gracious and merciful...
And His mercies are over all His works.
All Your works shall give thanks to You, O Lord,
And Your godly ones shall bless You.

PSALM 145:8-10

O God, we praise You and thank You

for mercy so undeserved, and for grace beyond measure.

Your lovingkindness is inexhaustible;

Your mercies endure forever;

Your faithfulness extends to all generations;

Your glory is seen in all Your works;

and Your steadfast love is our song.

We come to You, the Almighty God,

enthroned in our lives,

presiding over the universe,

and we humbly ask for You to strengthen us where we are weak,

beginning with our acts of worship.

You who spoke the universe into existence with but a word

are the One who has shone in our hearts

to give the Light of the knowledge of the glory of God

in the face of Christ.

How we thank You again for commanding salvation on our behalf!

Lord, we come before You in prayer to bring You our praise.

Set our lives in order before You,

and renew our commitment to love and obedience,

usefulness and faithfulness.

Be honored through our lives, we pray,

in the name of Christ. Amen.

O worship the King, all glorious above,
O gratefully sing His power and His love;
Our Shield and Defender, the Ancient of Days,
Pavilioned in splendor, and girded with praise.

ROBERT GRANT

When we offer praise to God, we approach in our worship on
earth the nearest to the worship of the glorified in heaven.

OCTAVIUS WINSLOW

His All-Encompassing Love

O Lord, You have searched me and known me.
You know when I sit down and when I rise up;
You understand my thought from afar.
You scrutinize my path and my lying down,
And are intimately acquainted with all my ways.

PSALM 139:1-3

Heavenly Father,

    it is such a staggering realization to understand that You,

    the infinite God of the universe, truly love us—

    with a love that is everlasting.

You set that love on us before time began.

You chose us and ordained us to eternal life

    in timeless ages past,

    and therefore we rest in the assurance

      that Your love will endure

        into the countless ages of eternity future.

So many tokens of Your goodness and mercy encourage us
 amid the discouraging realities of life in this fallen world.
When we become downhearted,
 You give us sympathy and support in abundant measure.
When we face grave temptations,
 You are our Guardian and refuge.
 You strengthen us in the hour of trial;
 and in the wake of every victory
  You lead us in triumph.
You never cease to love us;
 You never fail to preserve us.
You have promised never to leave or forsake us;
 You are with us—and in us—forever.

Oh God our Help in ages past,
Our Hope for years to come,
Be Thou our Guide while life shall last,
And our eternal Home!

ISAAC WATTS

Shall light troubles make you forget weighty mercies?

JOHN FLAVEL

Loving with a Heavenly Love

Owe nothing to anyone except to love one another.

ROMANS 13:8

Gracious Father, anyone who does not love does not truly know You,
because You are a God of love.
The sum of Your commandments is love.
All that You require of us is that we love You
with all our heart, soul, mind, and strength,
and love others as ourselves.

And yet, Lord, we fall far short of loving You as we should.
Love for self too often overwhelms our love for one another.
Even the best of our love is but a faint glimmer
of what it ought to be.

The Majesty of Prayer

We stand in desperate need of daily grace and forgiveness,
and we confess that apart from Your mercy to us
we would be utterly without hope.
It is our blessed privilege as Your children
to come boldly to the throne of grace again and again,
where we always receive mercy and find grace to help
in time of need.
We come therefore to worship You
as those who live by Your love.
May Your love be the mold that shapes
our actions, our words,
our character, and our very lives
so the whole world may see and honor You.
We pray in His precious name. Amen.

I love Thee, because Thou has first loved me,
And purchased my pardon on Calvary's tree;
I love Thee for wearing the thorns on Thy brow;
If ever I loved Thee, my Jesus, 'tis now.

WILLIAM RALPH FEATHERSTONE

God loves each of us as if there were only one of us.
SAINT AUGUSTINE

The God of All Comfort

Why are you in despair, O my soul?
And why have you become disturbed within me?
Hope in God, for I shall again praise Him
For the help of His presence.

PSALM 42:5

Our Father, life in this sin-cursed world
    sometimes seems full of anguish—
    and we are too prone to fatigue and discouragement.
As Your children, we thirst for You and trust in You deep down.
We long to sense Your presence.
We need Your tender mercy.
We crave Your heavenly comfort.
We stand in awe of Your wisdom,
    Your faithfulness,
    and Your perfect timing.
Our experience confirms the testimony of Your Word:
    You have never forsaken us.

Thus with settled confidence

    we echo the bold expectancy of the psalmist:

      We shall yet praise You.

Bearing in mind those precious truths,

    we approach Your throne once again

      with both fearful trembling and holy boldness.

You are both glorious and merciful;

    almighty and full of compassion;

    a righteous Judge but extravagant with tender mercies.

We seek Your blessed favor in our times of need,

    although we know we are unworthy,

    because You have summoned us

      to come confidently to the throne of grace.

Afflictions, they are but our Father's goldsmiths working to add pearls to our crowns.

THOMAS BROOKS

Nothing is so calming and comforting to the Christian pilgrim as the assurance of
Divine Guidance in every, even most minute circumstances, that befall him.

THOMAS READE

One Almighty is more than all mighties.
WILLIAM GURNALL

The First and the Last

I am the Alpha and the Omega, the first and
the last, the beginning and the end.

REVELATION 22:13

We love You, O Lord, our strength.

You are all glorious, all powerful, all knowing,

    all wise, all gracious, and all sufficient.

You are the Alpha and Omega,

    the first and the last, the beginning and the end.

All glory, honor, and power belong to You,

    and You alone are worthy to be praised;

    because You created all things,

    and because of Your will and for Your sake

      they were created.

All knowledge belongs to You.

All wisdom originates with You.

No one ever gave You direction or counsel;

    no one ever instructed You in the way of understanding.

Humanity is like a drop from a bucket and a speck of dust on the scales.

All the nations are nothing before You—

    less than nothing. Meaningless.

No one and nothing compares to You.

We celebrate Your goodness, Lord,

    and we praise You for Your grace toward us,

    confessing that we are completely unworthy of such favor.

We are overwhelmed when we contemplate our iniquities and failures,

    knowing we fall far short

        of that righteousness with which we have been covered:

          the righteousness of Christ credited to our account.

That is why we come before You now:

    to worship You, to proclaim Your truth,

    to sing Your praises, to be confronted by Your Word,

    and to be conformed to the image of Christ,

        in whose name we pray. Amen.

God has all the power that is consistent with infinite perfection.
AUGUSTUS H. STRONG

Far above all finite comprehension is the unchanging faithfulness of God.
Everything about God is great, vast, incomparable. He never forgets,
never fails, never falters, never forfeits His word.
ARTHUR WALKINGTON PINK

A Father Like No Other

What we have seen and heard we proclaim to you also,
so that you too may have fellowship with us; and indeed our
fellowship is with the Father, and with His Son Jesus Christ.

1 JOHN 1:3

We thank You, heavenly Father,

for the glories of the gospel of our Lord Jesus Christ,

especially the fellowship we enjoy together

with You and Your Son.

Our tongues cannot find sufficient praise wherewith to bless You.

What You have done for us exceeds all human accolades.

Our poor minds can't begin to fathom the immensity of Your grace,

but we know that You are far more worthy

than human language could ever express.

That cannot stop us from trying—

and we trust that You will receive

the simple thanks of Your children.

Thank You for the daily mercies You shower us with:

the comforts and blessings of life,

the joy of family and friends,

the love of the church,

and countless other good things

that You give us richly to enjoy.

Thank You for the grace that is in Christ Jesus, our Savior.

Thank You for the great love

with which You drew us to Yourself.

Such divine favor is something we could never earn;

You have given it simply because we asked in faith

that You Yourself graciously supplied.

We cling to Christ, in whose name we pray,

asking in conclusion that through Him

we might bring honor to Your worthy name. Amen.

Live near to God and all things will appear little to you
in comparison with eternal realities.

ROBERT MURRAY M'CHEYNE

Unending Grace

We know love by this, that He laid down His life for us.

1 JOHN 3:16

Father, we are profoundly indebted

      for the grace You pour out upon us at all times.

It encourages us not to grow weary in our trials.

It calms our fears.

It removes our guilt.

It unfetters us from shame.

It strengthens us in our infirmities.

Thank You that this grace

      restores, leads, guards,

      supplies, and strengthens us.

It also encourages our hope in a world of difficulty.

Although once poor we are now rich,

      once bound we are now free,

      once defeated we are now triumphant.

———◇⊗◇———

Our duties call for more grace than we possess,

>   but not more than is found in You.

Help us, dear Lord, to experience all You would have for us—

>   whether prosperity or adversity,

>   loss or gain,

>   darkness or light,

>   sickness or health,

>   blessing or suffering.

May we follow joyfully wherever Christ leads us,

>   knowing Your providence is at work in it all,

>   Your purposes will be fulfilled,

>   and Your grace is always sufficient.

In that confidence we come before Your throne

>   to offer these petitions in the exalted name of Christ. Amen.

———◇⊗◇———

My future is as bright as the promises of God.

ADONIRAM JUDSON

———◇⊗◇———

All God's giants have been weak men who did great things for God
because they reckoned on God being with them.

J. HUDSON TAYLOR

The Christian life starts with grace, it must continue
with grace, it ends with grace. Grace, wondrous grace.
D. MARTYN LLOYD-JONES

A New Creation

If anyone is in Christ, he is a new creature; the old
things passed away; behold, new things have come.

2 CORINTHIANS 5:17

How thankful we are for Christ's work

    and Your Spirit enabling us to put our trust in Jesus as Lord!

In the moment we first believed, You granted us

    a new life, a new heart, and new, holy affections.

Thus regenerated, we now have by Your gracious hand a new capacity

    to do what is good, honorable, and righteous.

We praise You that in Christ

    we have been made capable of pleasing You.

In what better way can we thank You,

    and for what greater end have we been made?

With humility we seek always to remember

    that the will and the power to do right

        come only from You.

Help us to put off the old things and put on the new—

    and be renewed in the spirit of our minds.

May we faithfully follow the humble example of our Lord.

May we love Him sincerely,

    glory in His cross,

    pursue what is holy,

    and live in a way

        that presents Jesus Christ as all-glorious

        and draws those who don't know Him to seek Him.

These things we pray in His name. Amen.

How vast the treasures we possess!
How rich thy bounty, King of grace!
The world is ours, and worlds to come;
Earth is our lodge, and heaven our home.

ISAAC WATTS

There is an infinite fullness in Jesus Christ.

J.C. RYLE

Christ is the ocean, in which every drop is infinite compassion.
He is the mountain towering above the mountains,
in which every grain is God's own goodness.

HENRY LAW

All-Sufficient Grace

My grace is sufficient for you, for power is perfected in weakness.

2 CORINTHIANS 12:9

You know, dear Lord, that our lives here on earth
    are full of burdens, heartaches, and disappointments.
You permit those things to use them for our benefit.
May we bear them with grace and courage.
We thank You for the grace that sustains us
    in the midst of all our troubles.
We pray that through the trials You send our way
    You will keep our hearts filled
        with that peace which surpasses all comprehension
        and guards our hearts and minds in Christ Jesus.

The Majesty of Prayer

Thank You that when we falter or fail,

    You always restore us.

You give us grace upon grace without measure.

You abundantly supply every need we have.

Your grace is sufficient for all these things,

    and Your truth strengthens us for all things.

We bow our hearts to worship You

    in Your Son's blessed name. Amen.

One of the strongest and sweetest consolations God gives to His
sick and afflicted ones is the assurance that He not only knows their
sorrows, and tenderly sympathizes with them in their griefs, but that the
appointment of the trial proceeds from Him, and that its whole course
and continuance are watched by Him with infinite love and care.

SUSANNAH SPURGEON

If all stars withdraw their light while you are on the way
of God, assure yourselves that the sun is ready to rise.

JOHN OWEN

Grace can neither be bought, earned, or won by the creature.
If it could be, it would cease to be grace.

ARTHUR WALKINGTON PINK

Celebrating His Great Mercy

Blessed be the God and Father of our Lord Jesus Christ,
who according to His great mercy has caused us to be born again
to a living hope through the resurrection of Jesus Christ from the dead.

1 PETER 1:3

Lord, we thank You that You are faithful and just to forgive.

We are prompted from hearts transformed at our salvation

to run to You and embrace You with glad surrender.

Help us, Lord, to be earnest and honest in self-examination,

and in that exercise may Your Spirit

testify together with our spirit

that we are true children of our heavenly Father,

born again to a living hope.

Grant us grace that the fruit of regeneration

will flourish and multiply in our lives.

May our tears be tears of true repentance;

may our hope be grounded solely in Your Word;

may our works be energized by love;

and may our faith endure to the end of time!

All the compassions of all the tender fathers in the world compared with the tender mercies of our God would be but as a candle to the sun or a drop to the ocean.

MATTHEW HENRY

Take notice not only of the mercies of God, but of God in the mercies.

RALPH VENNING

He Is Our Everything

God is able to make all grace abound to you,
so that always having all sufficiency in everything,
you may have an abundance for every good deed.

2 CORINTHIANS 9:8

You, Lord, are everything we need;

    may we desire nothing more.

You are our stronghold and our Deliverer.

You are our strength and our hope.

You are our Guide and our Keeper.

You are the one true God, and the Rock of our salvation.

All Your grace abounds to us;

    we always have full sufficiency in everything.

Indeed, we have an abundance for every good deed.

May we not squander such exquisite blessings.

Cleanse us, so that we might more clearly reflect

    the glory of Christ.

Help us, even now, to give more perfect expression

    to the praise that will occupy our hearts throughout all eternity.

As always, we bring all these petitions in His blessed name.

May they be heard and answered

    as they are consistent with Your will. Amen.

The excellency of Christ is…an infinite excellency
…and the more the mind is used to it, the more excellent it
appears. Every new discovery makes this beauty more ravishing,
and the mind sees no end; here is room enough for the mind to
go deeper and deeper, and never come to the bottom.

JONATHAN EDWARDS

It is the happiness of heaven to have God be all in all.

JEREMIAH BURROUGHS

Reflecting His Love

Fervently love one another from the heart.

1 PETER 1:22

Almighty God, we are privileged to call You *our* Father.

You loved us and saved us and adopted us

into Your own family.

You have therefore called us as believers

to love one another with pure hearts fervently.

That includes not showing partiality,

which is one important way of fulfilling the royal law

of loving our neighbors as ourselves.

May our actions toward one another reflect the perfect love

with which You first loved us.

We take to heart how Christ taught us to pray,

    yearning for Your name to be hallowed,

    Your kingdom to come,

    and Your will to be done on earth as it is in heaven.

Those are the true desires of our hearts;

    forgive us for being so preoccupied with lesser things.

And yet You also invite us to ask You for our temporal needs—

    our daily bread and other needs, all of which You richly supply.

Always You answer with surpassingly more abundance

    than we have faith to ask or think.

We drink our fill of that abundance;

    and You keep it flowing like a river.

For with You is the fountain of life; in Your light we see light.

May we never forget how dependent we are

    on Your generous bounty;

    give us truly grateful hearts, and fill our mouths with praise.

The love of God abides forever the same. Since you have
known Him, He has never varied in His love for you.

C.H. SPURGEON

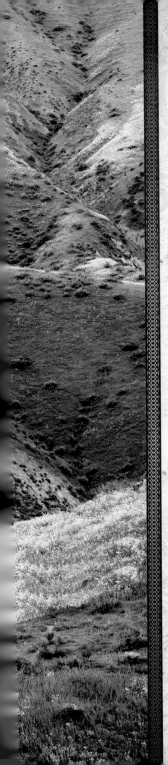

God's Greatest Gift

A child will be born to us…and His name will be called Wonderful
Counselor, Mighty God, Eternal Father, Prince of Peace.

ISAIAH 9:6

How could we ever thank You enough

> for sending Your own dear Son from heaven to earth

> in the form of a lowly,

> common-born human baby to be our Redeemer and Substitute?

The fullness of His condescension and sacrifice,

> His humble obedience to the point of death—

> even death on a cross—

> is beyond our mind's grasp.

It makes us eager for the time

> when every knee will bow and every tongue will confess

> > that Jesus Christ is Lord to Your glory, Father.

Heaven awaits a more suitable tribute

    than we are now capable of offering,

    and it will be our joy to fill all eternity with unbounded praise.

Our hearts are humbled and our minds taken captive

    by the reality that Christ left the glory of heaven

        to enter the world of humanity in so humble a fashion.

He was born like us, so that we might become like Him.

He made Himself a servant to show us how to lead.

He gave His life that we might live.

He suffered so that we can share in His glory.

In response we can only offer our highest words of praise—

    knowing how utterly feeble our best worship is,

    compared to the matchless worth of Christ.

Give us more suitable expressions of gratitude.

Fill us with hope and assurance.

Steady our erratic and error-prone walk.

Conform us to Christ's likeness and help us to walk in His steps.

And may our lives thus honor Him better

    than our tongues are able.

We ask these things in His blessed name. Amen.

In Christ Jesus heaven
meets earth and earth
ascends to heaven.

HENRY LAW

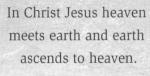

We are never nearer to Christ
than when we find ourselves
lost in a holy amazement
at His unspeakable love.

JOHN OWEN